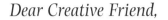

Dear Creative Friend,

Over the centuries, shawls have come to symbolize shelter, peace, and spiritual sustenance. Since the inception of The Prayer Shawl Ministry in 1998, the members of this ecumenical organization have lovingly donated their time and talents by creating hand-knitted and crocheted shawls for those in need. What started as a grass-roots movement has quickly grown into an international cause, with countless numbers of shawls being given to grateful recipients around the globe.

The ministry's message of caring is simple, universal, and enduring. And we have seen time and again that the creation and presentation of a prayer shawl, like all acts of generosity, enriches the giver as well as the recipient.

Lion Brand Yarn Company is honored to participate in this noble endeavor. The beautiful colors and silky softness of Lion Brand Homespun Yarn have made it the yarn of choice for many people who create prayer shawls. For this reason, Homespun yarn was used to create the shawls, stoles, and scarves featured as projects in this book. We have asked our friends at Leisure Arts to give you a closer look at this worthwhile ministry. In these pages, you will also find all the information you need to make the creation of prayer shawls a part of your life.

Hundreds of people have already shared their prayer shawl stories with us. We invite you to read their messages of hope and healing, and to share your own prayer shawl story at our website, www.lionbrand.com/shawlstories/html.

Lion Brand Yarn Company

1

EDITORIAL STAFF

Vice President and Editor-in-Chief: Sandra Graham Case. *Executive Director of Publications:* Cheryl Nodine Gunnells. *Senior Director of Publications:* Susan White Sullivan. *Director of Designer Relations:* Debra Nettles. *Director of Retail Marketing:* Stephen Wilson. *Art Operations Director:* Jeff Curtis. *Special Projects Coordinator:* Mary Sullivan Hutcheson. *Art Publications Director:* Rhonda Hodge Shelby. *Editorial Director:* Susan Frantz Wiles. *Art Imaging Director:* Mark Hawkins. *Technical Writer:* Linda Luder. *Editorial Writer:* Susan McManus Johnson. *Art Category Manager:* Rebecca J. Hester. *Imaging Technician:* Mark R. Potter. *Photographer:* Lloyd Litsey. *Photography Stylist:* Cassie Francioni. *Publishing Systems Administrator:* Becky Riddle. *Publishing Systems Assistants:* Clint Hanson, Josh Hyatt, and John Rose.

BUSINESS STAFF

Chief Operating Officer: Tom Siebenmorgen. *Vice President, Sales and Marketing:* Pam Stebbins. *Director of Sales and Services:* Margaret Reinold. *Vice President, Operations:* Jim Dittrich. *Comptroller, Operations:* Rob Thieme. *Retail Customer Service Manager:* Stan Raynor. *Print Production Manager:* Fred F. Pruss.

ACKNOWLEDGEMENTS

Lion Brand® Yarn Company and Leisure Arts, Inc., would like to thank the many individuals and churches who so graciously gave of their time and who shared with us their stories of inspiration and compassion:

Anne Russ, Pastor
Debbie Buckalew, Prayer Shawl Ministry Coordinator
Grace Presbyterian Church, Little Rock, Arkansas

Linda Fullerton, Prayer Shawl Ministry Coordinator
Grace United Methodist Church, Conway, Arkansas

Barbara Hickingbotham Wood, Prayer Shawl Ministry Coordinator
Immanuel Baptist Church, Little Rock, Arkansas

Margie Pulley, Owner
Bella Lana Knitting, Conway, Arkansas

Our thanks also go to Duncan & Nancy Porter and Dave & Kathi Jones, who allowed us to photograph our shawls in their homes.

Prayers on pages 14-17 are from *Prayers for Services*, compiled by Morgan Phelps Noyes, Copyright 1934 by Charles Scribner's Sons. Excerpt on page 18 from *Gates of Prayer for Shabbat and Weekdays*, Central Conference of American Rabbis, 1994, Chaim Stern, editor. Excerpt on page 18 from *Kol Haneshamah-Shabbat Vehagim*, 3rd ed., The Reconstructionist Press, 1996, David A. Teusch, editor.

Table *of Contents...*

A Tangible Evidence of Prayer 4
Letters to Lion Brand 8
Choosing Yarn Colors 12
    The Meanings of Colors 12
    Birthstone Colors 12
Prayers 14
    Before Working on a Shawl 14
    While Creating a Shawl For Healing 15
    For the Distressed 16
    For Those Who Mourn 17
    For Those Who Travel or Move Away 17
    A Jewish Shawl Blessing 18
    For a New Baby 19
    For a Graduate 19
    For Newlyweds 19
Crochet Patterns 20
    Rectangular Stole 20
    Small Throw 22
    Triangular Shawl 24
    Wide Scarf 26
Knit Patterns 28
    Rectangular Stole 28
    Small Throw 30
    Triangular Shawl 32
    Wide Scarf 34
Prayer Shawl Journal 36
General Instructions 38
    Abbreviations 38
    Gauge 38
    Basic Crochet Stitches & Techniques 39
    Basic Knit Stitches & Techniques 41

A Tangible *Evidence of P*

On a pleasant Sunday in the month of May, a small group of worshippers enters the central building of Grace Presbyterian Church in Little Rock, Arkansas. No one hurries to find a place in the pews. Instead, the members linger in the aisles of the neat, modest-sized sanctuary. They greet visitors and chat with friends and family. Several conversations are sprinkled with words that hint at an unusual activity taking place here at the church: *casting on, purling, fringe.* Not until the pianist plays the first reverent notes of the Call to Worship does silence fall over the gathering.

Prayer Shawls ready for blessing on the altar of Grace Presbyterian Church, Little Rock, Arkansas.

About midway through the Sunday service, Pastor Anne Russ steps behind the long altar. The curved rail is swathed in a rainbow of soft-looking fabrics. Pastor Russ observes the colorful display and waits for all eyes to find her. She is a picture of serenity and joy, even though the next half-hour will be filled with the serious matters of installing church elders, acknowledging college-bound students, and delivering her sermon.

But first, she must lead her congregation in a blessing.

"Because there are so many people in need of prayer, and because we want to do more than just say we are praying for them here at Grace Presbyterian Church, we have a prayer shawl ministry so that we are able to offer tangible evidence to those for whom we are praying."

Indicating the seven handmade shawls on the altar, Pastor Russ begins to name their intended recipients. With an appreciative smile, she also names the individuals who knitted or crocheted the shawls.

"I would like you to join me now," the pastor continues, "as we dedicate these prayer shawls, that they will be given to the recipients, and the blessings will not come just from the people who created them, not just from those who are part of the prayer shawl ministry, but from this entire congregation."

Pastor Russ begins the prayer: *Gracious, loving, and healing God, bless these shawls that they might be tangible evidence of the love and prayers of this congregation.*

And the people respond: *Bless the ones who will receive these shawls. Give them comfort, peace, healing, and strength. Remind them that they are loved and never forgotten. We ask your blessing on all who are lonely, sick, and suffering. In the name of Jesus Christ, the gentle healer. Amen.*

An inquisitive visitor to Grace Presbyterian will soon learn why the pastor is pleased by the work of her flock. Of those members who regularly attend services, one of every ten creates prayer shawls. The volunteers meet four times a month to work on

4

shawls and pray. Besides saying a group prayer at the start of each session, some of the individuals find that the repetitive nature of knitting or crocheting allows them to meditate and pray with every stitch. Many of them were strangers to needlework when the ministry began, including Pastor Russ. Her very first knitted item was a prayer shawl.

And it seems that Grace Presbyterian's prayer shawl ministry is growing beyond the borders of its membership. A crocheted shawl dedicated in today's service is from a visitor, a young man who wanted to take part in the blessing. Another shawl is a gift that arrived through the mail from an out-of-state aunt. She created it in the hope that it would be both moral support and spiritual protection for her college-bound niece.

Peter Beasley receives a prayer shawl from Virginia Robertson at Grace Presbyterian Church.

With all the interest surrounding Grace Presbyterian's newest ministry, it's difficult to believe it didn't exist just four months ago. Member Debbie Buckalew says, "Last January I read about prayer shawls in a newspaper article, and I knew immediately that it was exactly what I was looking for — a way to use creativity to reach out to people who are in need of comforting.

"I had just finished leading a children's class where we learned about a quilt that was passed from person to person as healing was needed. My goal in that class was to teach the children about compassionate ministry, but I had a need to get more involved myself."

Excited by the prospect of her church having its own prayer shawl ministry, Debbie made inquiries. Her search led her to Immanuel Baptist Church.

The members of Immanuel Baptist meet in an enormous red brick church that crowns a steep hill in west Little Rock. The spire of this shining edifice is visible for miles, but an hour with Barbara Hickingbotham Wood will assure anyone that the subject dearest to this church's congregation is not architecture.

Barbara is a retired employment counselor who now leads the Immanuel Baptist Prayer Shawl Ministry. She also teaches knitting, and with the help of other members of the ministry group, she delivers shawls to the critically ill members of the church, usually "home bound" individuals and nursing home patients.

The Immanuel group meets several times a month, and each meeting begins with "lots of conversation and excitement" while everyone notes the progress of each shawl and several new names are added to the list of intended recipients. When it's time to settle in and begin knitting, the work begins with prayer for every recipient on the list, including those who have already received shawls. Some knitters are also able to pray silently as they knit because the repetitive nature of the work requires little concentration.

"At our church," says Barbara, "we make shawls for the critically ill. We would like to add others to our list one day, maybe new mothers or newlyweds. But we have given 47 shawls so far, and we have an equal number of future recipients on our list. And all of these people are dealing with health issues."

Barbara's bright smile is momentarily tinged with sadness. "You see, I feel strongly that we must reach the very ill first, because not long ago I missed one. I was going to take a shawl to a lady the very next week, but she went to be with the Lord before I could get there. We have to concentrate on those whose health is frail or could become frail." The animation returning to her face, Barbara exclaims, "This ministry is my heartbeat! Let me show you why."

Barbara turns the pages of a binder filled with typewritten notes and snapshots. "This dear lady is Malinda. She is one-hundred-years-plus-six-months old. The extra six months are very important to her. She was widowed twice and says that caring for her husbands is why she is worn out now. Once we laid the shawl across her bed in the nursing home, she wouldn't let go of it. And she wouldn't let us rearrange it for her. She just kept patting it and saying, 'thank you, thank you, thank you.'

"This is Louise. She has diabetes and is wheelchair bound. We gave her a blue prayer shawl and she just

High school graduate Stephanie Martin receives a prayer shawl. Pastor Anne Russ of Grace Presbyterian Church presents the shawl, which was knitted by Stephanie's aunt.

loved it. It happened to match the color of her chair, her robe, and her eyes. She said even though her blood sugar was very high that morning, she felt much better with her shawl around her.

"Bill was so pleased to have people from his church come and visit him in the nursing home. He loved the prayer shawl and was overcome with appreciation and joy when we told him about the ministry. He said, 'You've really made my day.' "

Among the dozens of people who've received prayer shawls from the Immanuel volunteers are a young man with multiple sclerosis and a longtime choir member who can no longer attend church.

Of the former choir member, Barbara says, "She used to give candy to the children of the church and was blessed to receive a knitted 'treat' for herself."

In creating shawls and lap robes for the ill, the Immanuel group has made the recipients' comfort a priority. Barbara explains, "We only use Lion Brand Homespun because it is so very soft and washable. And we never knot the fringe that we add. If you are bedfast or can't move about frequently, then the knots could irritate your skin.

"We depend on donations from church members to pay for the yarn. Our knitters once modeled their shawls during a regular church event for women. This little 'fashion show' helped to raise an unusually large donation for our ministry, so this may be an idea that other churches will want to use to help with their work."

Thirty minutes west of Little Rock is the city of Conway. Margie Morse Pulley owns a popular yarn shop there, and she is an active member of the shawl ministry at her church, Grace United Methodist. "We find that making shawls together creates an environment of acceptance among the crafters. We've made shawls for healing, but we also make Celebration Shawls for happy occasions such as a student graduating high school or the arrival of a new baby. A new mom who is nursing finds a prayer shawl even more useful."

Says Linda Fullerton, also of Grace United Methodist in Conway, "When a shawl is for newlyweds, we usually make it larger than the normal shawl size, more like a throw for a couch. For individuals, one of our members prefers to make 'prayer ponchos.' Her arthritis makes knitting difficult, so she crochets them, sometimes finishing two or three a week! Because of her work

alone, we have a blessing ceremony almost every week."

At the end of the Sunday service at Grace Presbyterian Church, the newly blessed shawls are being presented to those recipients who are able to attend. It is evident that Debbie Buckalew's search for a ministry of compassion has ended with positive results for her church.

A gentleman in a wheelchair beams as a knitted shawl is placed around his shoulders. Pastor Russ acts as proxy for the loving aunt who could not attend, placing that lady's handiwork into the arms of her niece, a recent high school graduate.

And the young man who brought his crocheted shawl to be blessed now stands before the altar as his picture is taken. The soft blue-and-cream wrap rests in his creative hands for the last time. It will soon be a warm comfort — a tangible evidence of prayer — in the life of someone else.

Prayer Shawl creators at Grace Presbyterian Church with examples of the ministry's handiwork, from left to right: James Goodnight, Pastor Anne Russ, Mary Lynn Roberson, Betty Fulton, Janie Owen, and Virginia Robertson.

Letters to *Lion Brand*

In recent months, Lion Brand Yarn Company has received numerous letters and E-mails from knitters and crocheters who've discovered the rewarding ministry of prayer shawls. Their excitement is contagious as they describe the fulfillment their creativity brings them. Many of these kindhearted volunteers have also mentioned how much they enjoy working with Homespun yarn. We thought it would be inspiring to share a few of their letters with you.

A Prayer Shawl Ministry

I recently rediscovered my love of knitting when my friend Sue and I started a prayer shawl ministry at our church. Sue and I, both loving to do handiwork, wanted to create something that would benefit others. Separately, we became aware of shawls being used as a means to bring God's love, comfort, and peace to those in need. Sue had been to a wedding where a shawl was given. I attended a retreat and saw a prayer shawl being knitted.

Together, Sue and I excitedly discussed what we had learned. We both knew we had our answer! We took the idea to our pastors and our prayer shawl ministry was born.

Sue and I knit every day and can produce a shawl in less than a week. We have created and presented more than twenty shawls. We keep a yarn stockpile for future shawls. We use Lion Brand Homespun and Sue can now recite a color name by sight!

While our ministry is still in its infancy, others have begun to join us and we now have a total of six knitters and crocheters. We hope to gain more soon! Those in our church who don't knit/crochet have graciously provided us with donations of yarn or money to purchase yarn. Still others take our finished shawls and pray over them before they are given away.

This ministry has been extremely rewarding, knowing we are helping to provide "a hug from God" to those who are in need. Shawl recipients always comment on how soft and warm the yarn is, like God's love for us all!

I like the representation of intercessing to God, through my stitches, on another's behalf, and encourage anyone who loves to knit to begin a similar ministry whether through a church or as a community outreach program.

Knitting can truly be a wonderful ministry, for the recipient and the knitter alike!

A Homespun Yarn Fan

2 Learn, Knit, Give

In February of 2004, I made an announcement from the pulpit of my church. A fellow church member and I wanted to begin a prayer shawl ministry. Twelve people volunteered by the time we left church that day. Several of these volunteers did not know how to knit, so I held a couple of learning workshops before we started on the prayer shawls. Four of our members made their first shawls using only a knit stitch, as they were a bit leery of purl stitches at the early stage of learning. As of this writing, everyone has completed at least one shawl and is well into their second shawl. Some have knit four or more.

We meet once a month for meditation and conversation about those who need to receive a shawl. We usually have one or two to bless with our prayers and then we make a visit to the special someone who is to receive the shawl. We keep a log of who made the shawls and who received them.

We use Lion Brand Homespun yarn. We are very excited about the new colors.

Your Knitting Friends

Common Threads at St. Paul's Episcopal Church

We named our prayer shawl ministry group "Common Threads" because we ended up with not only several people who knit, but one wonderful woman, Pat, who cross-stitches pillowcases. Another woman, Kathy, is our only crocheter so far. And several of the teens in the church are turning out to be proficient knitters.

We have knit shawls for women who have sick or dying children. We have also made a lap robe for a male friend who is ill. We meet every three weeks to chat and knit, talk about new projects, compare notes, discuss yarns, and decide on future recipients. Almost all of our shawls have been made from your wonderful Homespun variety. Nothing in the world is softer.

We also have a ministry group that visits new mothers and helps them with advice and meals for the family. We have begun knitting baby caps for this ministry to deliver.

It is so fulfilling to know that something you made and that you prayed over with each stitch is so appreciated and loved by the recipient. To hear that a shawl is worn daily for comfort, for love, for consolation, or to see a brand-new baby wearing a cap made with love, there is nothing more rewarding.

We are able to use the talents God gave us to share His love with others. Isn't that the perfect mix?

Common Threads stitches on ...

Common Threads
Newnan, GA

9

Prayer Shawls

Dear People of Lion Brand:

I have knit since I was two years old. I was taught by my Auntie. I entered a baby set into the fair when I was five. I was awarded a blue ribbon, surprisingly!

Little did I know I was preparing for a ministry that would help so many people. I have made twelve prayer shawls that were blessed on the altar at our church and given to deserving people. I have gotten so much out of making and giving and praying for the recipients of these shawls. I have not only benefited spiritually while knitting, I relax this way and I believe it has helped relieve the arthritis that is trying to set in.

We have only used Lion Brand Homespun Yarn and the shawls turn out so soft you just want to curl up with one. Our hope is that each relieves the pain and suffering of the one we have prayed for while knitting, the one that receives each shawl.

Sincerely in His Love,

Kathy H.

A Prayer Shawl

A neighbor with breast cancer received a prayer shawl. I decided to look this up on the Internet.

I finally made one this past October for my grandma's birthday. I used Lion Brand Homespun in Delft, since blue is her favorite color. She is now eighty-eight and has asthma, chronic bronchitis and frequent bouts of pneumonia.

I sent her a card explaining the Trinity Stitch and the prayers I often repeated for her as I knit. She rarely uses the phone and even called me to say thank you and say that she didn't know that stitches could have stories.

I have another friend who is in need of comforting and I have purchased yarn for her shawl, too. I look forward to getting started on it soon.

A Prayer Shawl Partner

A Spirit Is Lifted

I have a friend who was diagnosed with cancer. She immediately went into a deep depression.

I decided to let her know that her friends were with her every step of the way. I crocheted a throw using Homespun in purple and pink worsted weight — the purple was for friendship and the pink was for love. I used a "V" for victory stitch throughout and, when it came time to put the fringe on, each one of her senior friends knotted a section onto the throw while saying a prayer for her recovery.

My friend's entire attitude changed when presented with the throw and she immediately cheered up, knowing, as she said, "that there are friends who care for me."

She has finished her chemo, has done well, stayed positive, and her Homespun victory throw buoys her up when she is down.

I would never have believed that such a small act of kindness would have made such a difference to anyone.

I encourage other people to do small acts of love like this. It benefits the giver as much as the recipient.

A Knitter

A Shawl of Light and Love

I knit every day, any spare minute I have. To my knowledge, there is not a [prayer shawl] group here.

I saw the article [about prayer shawls] in *Spirituality and Health Magazine*, then purchased the book *Knitting into the Mystery* [by Susan S. Jorgensen and Susan S. Izard]. I immediately purchased Homespun Yarn and was thrilled with the finished project.

The shawl was given to a lady in hospice care who may not be here for Christmas. When the shawl was placed on her, the light and love not only affected her but everyone who touched it.

I also make leg warmers, hats, gloves, scarves, etc., so at Christmas time I will deliver a lot more there.

I have knitted all my life and this is the most rewarding project I have ever done.

Thrilled with Homespun

letters

11

Choosing Yarn Colors

Lion Brand Homespun Yarn is currently available in over sixty colors, making it easy for you to choose yarn that's perfectly suited for the recipient of your shawl. Remember, for each shawl you wish to make, you will need sufficient yarn from a single dye lot. If you don't know the recipient's favorite color, here are two different methods for selecting yarn colors.

The Meanings of Colors

Whether you are creating a prayer shawl as a gift for healing, for protection, or for celebration, you may find a color that symbolizes the quality or sentiment you want your shawl to convey. Listed below are traditional meanings for several colors. If more than one color holds the meaning(s) you choose, consider using a variegated or "painterly" shade of Homespun Yarn that combines those colors.

COLOR	MEANINGS
Red	Energy, strength, power, determination, love, courage
Pink	Joy, friendship, femininity
Brown	Stability, masculinity
Orange	Happiness, success, encouragement, endurance
Gold	Illumination, wisdom
Yellow	Cheerfulness, energy, joy, confidence
Green	Healing, harmony, safety, hope, protection, peace
Blue	Stability, trust, loyalty, faith, truth, tranquility
Purple	Wisdom, dignity, independence, creativity, mystery
White	Goodness, purity, innocence, faith, safety, light

Birthstone Colors

Another method for choosing yarn color is to base your selection on the recipient's birthstone color (see chart at right). Because natural gemstones often vary by a few shades, we are recommending more than one color of Homespun Yarn for many of the birth months.

MONTH	GEM	GEM COLOR	HOMESPUN COLOR(S)
January	Garnet	dark red	Antique 307
February	Amethyst	purple	Grape 386, Lavender Sachet 390, Gothic 334
March	Aquamarine	pale blue	Waterfall 329, Windsor 341
April	Diamond	clear	Hepplewhite 300
May	Emerald	green	Country 304
June	Pearl	cream	Deco 309
July	Ruby	bright red	Candy Apple 375, Covered Bridge 367, Fuchsia 385
August	Peridot	pale green	Florida Keys Green 369, Olive 378, Spring Green 389
September	Sapphire	dark blue	Montana Sky 368, Colonial 302
October	Opal	variegated	Quartz 362, Tudor 315
November	Topaz	yellow	Lemonade 388, Sunshine State 372
December	Turquoise	sky blue	Blue Sky 391

yarn

Prayers...

...Before Working on a Shawl

O God, who has included all commandments in the one commandment of love, w humbly pray that you will create in our hearts such a sincere love of one another, tha we may be children of our Father in heaven, and true disciples of Jesus Christ. Amen

Adapted

R.C. Jone

Almighty and Everlasting God who created us for yourself, grant us purity of heart and strength of purpose to know your will. In your light may we see life clearly, and in you service find perfect freedom. Amen. *Adapted*

John Watson

... While Creating a Shawl for Healing

Most holy, wise, and powerful Preserver of all your creatures, keep us in health of body and soundness of mind. Keep us in purity of heart and cheerfulness of spirit, in contentment with our lives and in charity with our neighbors. Strengthen us in our labors. Direct us in our difficulties. Defend us from our perils. Comfort us in our troubles. And care for our needs according to the riches of your grace in Christ Jesus our Lord. Amen. *Adapted*

The Book of Common Worship

God of all comfort, we commend to thy mercy all those upon whom any cross or tribulation is laid; all persons oppressed with poverty, sickness, or any infirmity of body or sorrow of mind. We pray for those who desire to be remembered in our prayers and for any such known only to ourselves, whom we name in our hearts before thee. May it please thee to show them thy fatherly kindness in the midst of affliction, that their hearts may turn unto thee, and receive perfect consolation and healing, and deliverance from their troubles, for Christ's sake. Amen. *Adapted*

John Calvin

O Father of mercies and God of all comfort, our only help in time of need; we humbly beseech thee to behold, visit, and relieve thy sick servant for whom our prayers are desired. Look upon him in thy mercy; comfort him with a sense of thy goodness; and give him patience under his affliction. In thy good time and using all wise means, restore him to health, and enable him to lead his life to thy glory; and grant that he may finally dwell with thee in life everlasting; through Jesus Christ our Lord. Amen.

Book of Common Worship

Prayers...

...for the Distressed

O You, who understands the frailty of the human heart, hear our prayers for those who have been unfortunate in life and bruised in spirit; those who have toiled without success. For those who have endured with no outside encouragement; those who have given up all earthly prospects to comfort the aged and care for the maimed; those who are lonely in heart, and those for whom we do not know what to ask, but you know, O Lover of Souls. Amen. *Adapted*

Acts of Devotion

... for Those Who Mourn

O Father of infinite compassion, God of all comfort, reveal yourself as the Light of Life to those who have been brought into the darkness of sorrow. Strengthen the hearts that faint under the heavy burden, and support them in the arms of your infinite love. May they know that in all their distress you care for them with unfailing tenderness. Wipe away all tears from their eyes; through Jesus Christ our Lord. Amen. *Adapted*

Book of Church Services

We pray for all who mourn. You know their sorrow. You know and are the comforter of your children. In taking, as in giving, your hand is the hand of a father. May they find peace in you, in the fellowship of your gracious spirit. May the veil be taken away, and a glimpse of the everlasting brightness alight their faces. Sweeten our adversities; and though we go down into the valley of the shadow of death, may we know that you are strengthening our souls, and that all things are working together for good to those who love you. *Adapted*

Rufus Ellis

... for Those Who Travel or Move Away

O Lord our God, who is everywhere, from whom no space or distance can ever separate us, we know that those who are apart from us are present with You. We pray that You will hold in Your holy keeping those dear ones from whom we are now separated. Grant that both we and they, by drawing nearer to You, will be drawn nearer to each other. Bind us together by the unseen chain of Your love in the communion of Your spirit, and in the holy fellowship of your saints. *Adapted*

Sir William Martin

Prayers...

... a Jewish Shawl Blessing

Bar-chi naf-shi et A-do-nai.
Praise the Eternal One, O my soul!
O God, You are very great!

Arrayed in glory and majesty, You wrap Yourself in light as with a garment, and stretch out the heavens like a curtain.

—from *Gates of Prayer for Shabbat and Weekday*

The commentary in the *Kol Haneshamah-Shabbat Vehagim* states that "God's wrapping in light becomes Israel's enlightened wrapping at the outset of a new day." May it be so for each of us.

Contributed by Anna Rose and Monte Sugarman
Taken from Shabbat Morning Service

... for a New Baby

Creator of all life, thank you for this new soul you have sent to us! Bless this little one with love and health, and protect him from all evil. Guide this precious child onto the path that leads to You. And give us wisdom to be the nurturers and teachers he needs us to be. Amen.

... for a Graduate

Father, there is nothing you do not know of this young woman. Protect her as she leaves behind the things of childhood to take her place in the world. Remind her daily of your love and caring. As she shoulders new responsibilities and reaches for her goals, strengthen her to seek your guidance in all things. Bless her with the fruit of her labors, and make her life a blessing to all. Amen.

... for Newlyweds

Heavenly Father, here is love as You have taught us it should be, that two should become one. We ask Your blessings on this man and this woman. Let their days together be long and fruitful. Do not let pride bring harm to their union, but let each one be a constant source of light for the other, just as You are the source of strength, joy, love, and peace for Your church. Amen.

prayers

Crochet Rectangular Stole

Finished Size: 30" x 72" (76 cm x 183 cm)

MATERIALS
Lion Brand® Homespun® **[BULKY 5]**
336 Barrington **or** color of your choice
6 skeins
Crochet hook, size K (6.5 mm) **or**
size needed for gauge

GAUGE: In pattern, 11 sts = $4^1/_4$" (10.75 cm);
8 rows = $4^1/_2$" (11.5 cm)

Gauge Swatch: $4^1/_4$" x $4^1/_2$"
(10.75 cm x 11.5 cm)
Ch 12.
Work same as Stole for 8 rows.
Finish off.

STOLE
Ch 72.

Row 1: Sc in second ch from hook and in each ch across: 71 sc.

Row 2: Ch 3 (counts as first dc), turn; dc in next sc, ★ ch 1, skip next sc, dc in next 2 sc; repeat from ★ across: 48 dc and 23 ch-1 sps.

Row 3: Ch 1, turn; sc in each dc and in each ch-1 sp across: 71 sc.

Repeat Rows 2 and 3 until Stole measures approximately 72" (183 cm) from beginning ch, ending by working Row 3.

Finish off.

Design by Shirley Evers.

patterns

20

Crochet Small Throw

Finished Size: 40" x 52" (101.5 cm x 132 cm)

MATERIALS
Lion Brand® Homespun®
326 Ranch **or** color of your choice
  6 skeins
Crochet hook, size K (6.5 mm) **or**
  size needed for gauge

GAUGE: In pattern, 18 sts = 7" (17.75 cm);
        8 rows = 5" (12.75 cm)

Gauge Swatch: 7"w x 5"h
             (17.75 cm x 12.75 cm)
Ch 19.
Work same as Afghan Body for 8 rows.
Finish off.

AFGHAN BODY
Ch 95.

Row 1 (Wrong side)**:** Sc in second ch from hook and in next ch, ★ ch 2 skip next 2 chs, sc in next 2 chs; repeat from ★ across: 48 sc and 23 ch-2 sps.

Note: Loop a short piece of yarn around **back** of any stitch on Row 1 to mark **right** side.

Row 2: Ch 3 **(counts as first dc, now and throughout)**, turn; 4 dc in each ch-2 sp across, skip next sc, dc in last sc: 94 dc.

Row 3: Ch 1, turn; sc in first 2 dc, ★ ch 2, skip next 2 dc, sc in next 2 dc; repeat from ★ across: 48 sc and 23 ch-2 sps.

Repeat Rows 2 and 3 until Afghan Body measures approximately 48$^{1}/_{2}$" (131 cm) from beginning ch, ending by working Row 3; do **not** finish off.

EDGING
Rnd 1: Ch 1, turn; 2 sc in each of first 2 sc and in next ch-2 sp, (sc in next 2 sc, 2 sc in next ch-2 sp) across to last 2 sc, sc in next sc, 3 sc in last sc; work 123 sc evenly spaced across end of rows; working in sps and in free loops of beginning ch *(Fig. 7, page 40)*, 3 sc in ch at base of first sc, 2 sc in next ch and in next sp, (sc in next 2 chs, 2 sc in next sp) across to last 2 chs, sc in next ch, 3 sc in last ch; work 123 sc evenly spaced across end of rows, sc in same st as first sc; join with slip st to first sc: 444 sc.

Rnd 2 (Eyelet rnd)**:** Ch 4 **(counts as first dc plus ch 1)**, do **not** turn; dc in same st, ch 1, ★ (skip next sc, dc in next sc, ch 1) across to next corner 3-sc group, skip next sc, (dc, ch 1) twice in center sc; repeat from ★ 2 times **more**, skip next sc, (dc in next sc, ch 1, skip next sc) across; join with slip st to first dc: 226 dc and 226 ch-1 sps.

Rnd 3: Ch 1, sc in same st, 3 sc in next corner ch-1 sp, sc in each dc and in each ch-1 sp around working 3 sc in each corner ch-1 sp; join with slip st to first sc: 460 sc.

Rnd 4: Ch 1, sc in same st, ch 3, skip next sc, ★ sc in next sc, ch 3, skip next sc; repeat from ★ around; join with slip st to first sc, finish off.

Design by Joyce Sandra Abbate.

Crochet Triangular Shawl

EASY

Finished Size: 65" wide x 33" deep
(165 cm x 84 cm)

MATERIALS

Lion Brand® Homespun® **[BULKY 5]**
301 Shaker **or** color of your choice
4 skeins
Crochet hook, size K (6.5 mm) **or**
size needed for gauge

GAUGE: In pattern, four 3-dc groups
and 7 rows = $4^3/_4$" (12 cm)

Gauge Swatch: $5^1/_4$" x $7^3/_4$" x $5^1/_4$"
(13.25 cm x 19.75 cm x 13.25 cm)
Work same as Shawl for 4 rows.

SHAWL

Row 1: Ch 7, (3 dc, ch 1, 3 dc) in fourth ch from hook, skip next 2 chs, slip st in next ch: two 3-dc groups and one ch-1 sp.

Row 2: Ch 4, turn; 3 dc in sp **before** next 3-dc group *(Fig. A)*, (3 dc, ch 1, 3 dc) in next ch-1 sp, skip next 3-dc group, 3 dc in sp **before** beginning ch, dc in top of beginning ch: four 3-dc groups and one ch-1 sp.

Fig. A

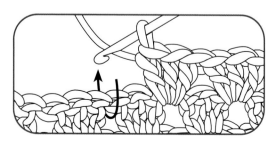

Row 3: Ch 4, turn; skip first dc, 3 dc in sp **before** each of next two 3-dc groups, (3 dc, ch 1, 3 dc) in next ch-1 sp, skip next 3-dc group, 3 dc in sp **before** next 3-dc group and in sp **before** turning ch, dc in third ch of turning ch: six 3-dc groups and one ch-1 sp.

Row 4: Ch 4, turn; skip first dc, 3 dc in sp **before** next 3-dc group and in sp **before** each 3-dc group across to next ch-1 sp, (3 dc, ch 1, 3 dc) in ch-1 sp, skip next 3-dc group, 3 dc in sp **before** next 3-dc group and in sp **before** each 3-dc group across, 3 dc in sp before turning ch, dc in third ch of turning ch: eight 3-dc groups and one ch-1 sp.

Repeat Row 4 until Shawl measures approximately $62^1/_2$" (159 cm) wide **or** $2^1/_2$" (6.5 cm) less than desired width; do **not** finish off.

TRIM

Foundation Rnd: Ch 1; sc evenly in end of rows across long edge of Shawl; ch 5, skip next 3-dc group, (sc in sp **before** next 3-dc group, ch 5) across to next ch-1 sp, sc in ch-1 sp, ch 5, skip next 3-dc group, (sc in sp **before** next 3-dc group, ch 5) across; join with slip st to first sc.

Row 1 (Wrong side): Ch 5, turn; sc in first ch-5 sp, ch 5, (sc in next ch-5 sp, ch 5) across, sc in next sc; leave remaining sc unworked.

Rows 2 and 3: Ch 5, turn; sc in first ch-5 sp, ch 5, (sc in next ch-5 sp, ch 5) across to last ch-5 sp, sc in center ch of last ch-5 sp.

Finish off.

Design by Jan Corbally.

patterns

Crochet Wide Scarf

Finished Size: 18" x 72" (45.5 cm x 183 cm)

MATERIALS
Lion Brand® Homespun®
341 Windsor **or** color of your choice
4 skeins
Crochet hook, size K (6.5 mm) **or**
size needed for gauge

GAUGE: 5 V-Sts and 7 rows = 5¹/₂" (14 cm)

Gauge Swatch: 6"w x 5¹/₂"h
(15.25 cm x 14 cm)
Ch 21.
Work same as Scarf for 7 rows.
Finish off.

SCARF
FIRST HALF
Ch 51, place marker in third ch from hook to mark st placement.

Row 1 (Right side): (Dc, ch 2, dc) in sixth ch from hook, ★ skip next 2 chs, (dc, ch 2, dc) in next ch; repeat from ★ across to last 3 chs, skip next 2 chs, dc in last ch: 32 sts and 15 ch-2 sps.

Note: Loop a short piece of yarn around any stitch to mark Row 1 as **right** side.

Row 2: Ch 3 (**counts as first dc, now and throughout**), turn; (dc, ch 2, dc) in each ch-2 sp across to last dc, skip last dc, dc in next ch: 32 dc and 15 ch-2 sps.

Row 3: Ch 3, turn; (dc, ch 2, dc) in each ch-2 sp across to last 2 dc, skip next dc, dc in last dc.

Repeat Row 3 until piece measures approximately 36" (91.5 cm) from beginning ch.

Finish off.

SECOND HALF
With **right** side facing and working in free loops of beginning ch (*Fig. 7, page 40*), join yarn with slip st in first ch; ch 3, skip next 2 chs, ★ (dc, ch 2, dc) in next ch, skip next 2 chs; repeat from ★ across to marked ch, dc in marked ch: 32 dc and 15 ch-2 sps.

Repeat Row 3 of First Half until Second Half measures approximately 36" (91.5 cm) from beginning ch [Shawl should measure a total of 72" (183 cm)].

Finish off.

patterns

Knit Rectangular Stole

Finished Size: 34" x 72" (86.5 cm x 183 cm)

MATERIALS

Lion Brand® Homespun®
346 Bella Vista **or** color of your choice
  5 skeins
29" (73.5 cm) Circular knitting needle,
  size 13 (9 mm) **or** size needed for gauge

GAUGE: One pattern repeat
    (20 sts) = 7³/₄" (19.75 cm);
    8 rows = 2¹/₄" (5.75 cm)
    In Garter Stitch,
    10 sts and 16 rows = 4" (10 cm)

Gauge Swatch: 4" (10 cm) square
Cast on 10 sts.
Knit 16 rows.
Bind off all sts in **knit**.

STOLE

Cast on 87 sts.

Rows 1-10: Knit across.

Row 11 (Right side)**:** K 11, P5, (K 15, P5) 3 times, K 11.

Row 12: K6, P5, K5, (P 15, K5) 3 times, P5, K6.

Row 13: K 11, P5, (K 15, P5) 3 times, K 11.

Row 14: Knit across.

Row 15: K 21, P5, (K 15, P5) twice, K 21.

Row 16: K6, P 15, (K5, P 15) 3 times, K6.

Row 17: K 21, P5, (K 15, P5) twice, K 21.

Row 18: Knit across.

Repeat Rows 11-18 for pattern until Stole measures approximately 70" (178 cm) from cast on edge, ending by working Row 13.

Last 11 Rows: Knit across.

Bind off all sts in **knit**.

Design by John Feddersen, Jr.

Knit Small Throw

Finished Size: 41$^1/_2$" x 54" (105.5 cm x 137 cm)

MATERIALS

Lion Brand® Homespun®
370 Coral Gables **or** color of your choice
  5 skeins
29" (73.5 cm) Circular knitting needle,
  size 13 (9 mm) **or** size needed for gauge

GAUGE: One pattern (15 sts) and
14 rows = 5" (12.75 cm)

Gauge Swatch: 6$^1/_2$"w x 5"h
(16.5 cm x 12.75 cm)
Cast on 19 sts.
Work same as Afghan Body for 13 rows.
Bind off all sts in pattern.

AFGHAN BODY

Cast on 124 sts.

Row 1 (Right side)**:** K2, ★ K2 tog *(Fig. 13, page 44)*, K5, YO *(Fig. 12a, page 43)*, K1, YO, K5, [slip 1, K1, PSSO *(Figs. 14a & b, page 44)*]; repeat from ★ across to last 2 sts, K2.

Row 2: K2, purl across to last 2 sts, K2.

Row 3: K2, ★ K2 tog, K5, YO, K1, YO, K5, slip 1, K1, PSSO; repeat from ★ across to last 2 sts, K2.

Repeat Rows 2 and 3 for pattern until Afghan Body measures approximately 54" (137 cm) from cast on edge, ending by working Row 2.

Bind off all sts in **knit**.

FRINGE

Cut a piece of cardboard 6" (15 cm) wide and 8" (20.5 cm) long. Wind the yarn **loosely** and **evenly** lengthwise around the cardboard until the card is filled, then cut across one end; repeat as needed. Hold 8 strands of yarn together; fold in half. With **wrong** side facing and using a crochet hook, draw the folded end up through a point on short edge of Afghan Body and pull the loose ends through the folded end *(Fig. A)*; draw the knot up **tightly** *(Fig. B)*. Repeat, in each point and between points across short edges of Afghan Body.

Fig. A   **Fig. B**

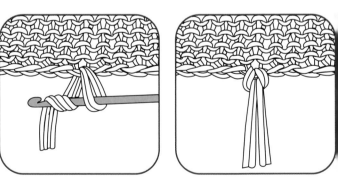

Design by John Feddersen, Jr.

Knit Triangular Shawl

Finished Size: 65" wide x 33" deep
(165 cm x 84 cm)

MATERIALS

Lion Brand® Homespun®
322 Baroque **or** color of your choice
3 skeins
29" (73.5 cm) Circular knitting needle,
size 13 (9 mm) **or** size needed for gauge

GAUGE: In Garter Stitch,
10 sts and 16 rows = 4" (10 cm)

Gauge Swatch: 4" (10 cm) square
Cast on 10 sts.
Knit 16 rows.
Bind off all sts in **knit**.

SHAWL

Cast on one st.

Row 1: Knit into the front **and** into the back of st
(Figs. A & B, **increase made**): 2 sts.

Fig. A   Fig. B

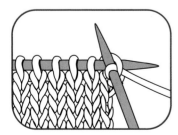   

Row 2: Increase, K1: 3 sts.

Rows 3-6: Increase, knit across: 7 sts.

Rows 7: K3, YO *(Fig. 12a, page 43)*, knit across:
8 sts.

Repeat Row 7 until piece measures approximately
32" (81.5 cm) from cast on edge, ending with an
even number of stitches.

Next Row: K3, YO, ★ K2 tog *(Fig. 13, page 44)*,
YO; repeat from ★ across to last 3 sts, K3.

Next 4 Rows: Increase, knit across.

Bind Off Row: K2 tog, ★ K1, pass second st on
right needle over first st; repeat from ★ across to
last 2 sts, K2 tog, pass second st on right needle
over first st and finish off.

Design by John Feddersen, Jr.

Knit Wide Scarf

Finished Size: 18" x 72" (45.5 cm x 183 cm)

MATERIALS
Lion Brand® Homespun® **BULKY 5**
385 Fuchsia **or** color of your choice
  4 skeins
Straight knitting needles, size 10 (6 mm) **or**
  size needed for gauge

GAUGE: In pattern, 14 sts = $4^{1}/_{4}$" (10.75 cm);
  18 rows = $3^{1}/_{4}$" (8.25 cm)

Gauge Swatch: $6^{1}/_{4}$"w x 4"h (16 cm x 10 cm)
Cast on 20 sts.
Work same as Scarf for 22 rows.
Bind off all sts in **purl**.

SCARF
Cast on 58 sts.

Rows 1-4: Purl across.

Row 5 (Right side): P3, ★ YO *(see Yarn Overs, page 43)*, K2 tog *(Fig. 13, page 44)*; repeat from ★ across to last 3 sts, P3.

Row 6: Purl across.

Row 7: P3, (K2 tog, YO) across to last 3 sts, P3.

Rows 8-10: Purl across.

Row 11: P3, (YO, K2 tog) across to last 3 sts, P3.

Repeat Rows 6-11 for pattern until Scarf measures approximately 71" (180.5 cm) from cast on edge, ending by working Row 7.

Last 4 Rows: Purl across.

Bind off all sts in **purl**.

FRINGE
Cut a piece of cardboard 6" (15 cm) wide and 8" (20.5 cm) long. Wind the yarn **loosely** and **evenly** around the cardboard lengthwise until the card is filled, then cut across one end; repeat as needed.

Step 1: Hold together 8 strands of yarn; fold in half. With **wrong** side facing and using a crochet hook, draw the loose ends through the folded end *(Fig. A)*; draw the knot up **tightly** *(Fig. B)*. Repeat spacing as desired.

Step 2: Divide each group in half and knot together with half of next group *(Fig. C)*.

Step 3: Separate each group in same manner and knot again *(Fig. D)*.

Step 4: Lay Scarf flat on a hard surface and trim the ends.

Fig. A   Fig. B

Fig. C   Fig. D

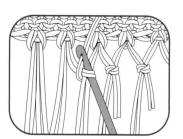

Barbara presented Sarah with her shawl on May 15, 2005. Sarah is 92 years young. Her keen sense of humor had everyone laughing. You never know what Sarah will say, but you know you want to be there when she says it.

Prayer Shawl Journal

A Prayer Shawl Ministry Journal is not only a lovely keepsake, it is a useful way to document your work. For example, if you wish to keep someone on your prayer list after that person receives a shawl, your journal will help you remember details about the recipient's health or other concerns. If you are keeping the journal for a group ministry, the documentation will also help new volunteers understand your outreach program.

Our sample pages show two different ways to document your ministry. Both are easy to make with scrapbook papers and stickers.

Date & Name

1.

Notes

2.

This shawl was hand[made]
for you by our Pr[ayer]
Shawl Ministry. As [it was]
created, we prayed [for you.]
We asked the Lord [to give]
you many bless[ings]
courage, strength, [...]
May this shawl wr[...]
comfort even as [...]

This shawl was [handmade]
for you by ou[r Prayer]
Shawl Minist[ry...]
created, we p[rayed...]
We asked t[he...]
[...] ma[...]

This shawl was handmade
for you by our Prayer
Shawl Ministry. As it was
created, we prayed for you.
We asked the Lord to give
you many blessings...
courag[e...]

[...]as handmade
[...] our Pra-
[...]

Immanuel Baptist Church
Prayer Shawl Ministry
Journal

Jesus said, "Therefore I say unto you, What things soever
ye desire, when ye pray, believe that ye receive them, and ye
shall have them."
Mark 11:24

journal

Presentation Cards

The presentation of a prayer shawl is a loving, caring gesture, and the shawl is a complete gift by itself. But if you wish to add a note along with your shawl, then a presentation card is a thoughtful way to convey your sentiments. With the use of a home computer or the services of your local print shop, creating these cards can be simple and inexpensive. Try using decorative papers and stickers to make your presentation tags special.

General Instructions

ABBREVIATIONS

ch(s)	chain(s)
cm	centimeters
dc	double crochet(s)
K	knit
mm	millimeters
P	purl
PSSO	pass slipped stitch over
Rnd(s)	Round(s)
sc	single crochet(s)
sp(s)	space(s)
st(s)	stitch(es)
tog	together
YO	yarn over

★ — work instructions following ★ as many **more** times as indicated in addition to the first time.

( ) or **[ ]** — work enclosed instructions **as many** times as specified by the number immediately following **or** work all enclosed instructions in the stitch or space indicated **or** contains explanatory remarks.

colon (:) — the number(s) given after a colon at the end of the row or round denote(s) the number of stitches or spaces you should have on that row or round.

GAUGE

Exact gauge is **essential** for proper size. Before beginning your project, make the sample swatch given in the individual instructions in the yarn, stitch and hook or needle specified. After completing the swatch, measure it, counting your stitches and rows/rounds carefully. If your swatch is larger or smaller than specified, **make another, changing hook or needle size to get the correct gauge**. Keep trying until you find the size hook or needle that will give you the specified gauge.

KNIT TERMINOLOGY	
UNITED STATES	**INTERNATIONAL**
gauge =	tension
bind off =	cast off
yarn over (YO) =	yarn forward (yfwd) **or**
	yarn around needle (yrn)

CROCHET TERMINOLOGY	
UNITED STATES	**INTERNATIONAL**
slip stitch (slip st) =	single crochet (sc)
single crochet (sc) =	double crochet (dc)
half double crochet (hdc) =	half treble crochet (htr)
double crochet (dc) =	treble crochet (tr)
treble crochet (tr) =	double treble crochet (dtr)
double treble crochet (dtr) =	triple treble crochet (ttr)
triple treble crochet (tr tr) =	quadruple treble crochet (qtr)
skip =	miss

CROCHET HOOKS													
U.S.	B-1	C-2	D-3	E-4	F-5	G-6	H-8	I-9	J-10	K-10½	N	P	Q
Metric - mm	2.25	2.75	3.25	3.5	3.75	4	5	5.5	6	6.5	9	10	15

KNITTING NEEDLES															
U.S.	0	1	2	3	4	5	6	7	8	9	10	10½	11	13	15	17
U.K.	13	12	11	10	9	8	7	6	5	4	3	2	1	00	000	---
Metric - mm	2	2.25	2.75	3.25	3.5	3.75	4	4.5	5	5.5	6	6.5	8	9	10	12.75

■□□□ BEGINNER	Projects for first-time knitters & crocheters using basic stitches. Minimal shaping.
■■□□ EASY	Projects using yarn with basic stitches, repetitive stitch patterns, simple color changes, & simple shaping & finishing.
■■■□ INTERMEDIATE	**CROCHET:** Projects using a variety of techniques, such as basic lace patterns or color patterns, mid-level shaping & finishing. **KNIT:** Projects with a variety of stitches, such as basic cables & lace, simple intarsia, double-pointed needles & knitting in the round needle techniques, mid-level shaping & finishing.
■■■■ EXPERIENCED	**CROCHET:** Projects with intricate stitch patterns, techniques & dimension, such as non-repeating patterns, multi-color techniques, fine threads, small hooks, detailed shaping & refined finishing. **KNIT:** Projects using advanced techniques & stitches, such as short rows, fair isle, more intricate intarsia, cables, lace patterns, & numerous color changes.

general instructions

Yarn Weight Symbol & Names	SUPER FINE 1	FINE 2	LIGHT 3	MEDIUM 4	BULKY 5	SUPER BULKY 6
Type of Yarns in Category	Sock, Fingering Baby	Sport, Baby	DK, Light Worsted	Worsted, Afghan, Aran	Chunky, Craft, Rug	Bulky, Roving
Crochet Gauge Ranges in Single Crochet to 4" (10 cm)	21-32 sts	16-20 sts	12-17 sts	11-14 sts	8-11 sts	5-9 sts
Advised Hook Size Range	B-1 to E-4	E-4 to 7	7 to I-9	I-9 to K-10.5	K-10.5 to M-13	M-13 and larger

Yarn Weight Symbol & Names	SUPER FINE 1	FINE 2	LIGHT 3	MEDIUM 4	BULKY 5	SUPER BULKY 6
Type of Yarns in Category	Sock, Fingering Baby	Sport, Baby	DK, Light Worsted	Worsted, Afghan, Aran	Chunky, Craft, Rug	Bulky, Roving
Knit Gauge Ranges in Stockinette St to 4" (10 cm)	27-32 sts	23-26 sts	21-24 sts	16-20 sts	12-15 sts	6-11 sts
Advised Needle Size Range	1-3	3-5	5-7	7-9	9-11	11 and larger

Basic Crochet Stitches & Techniques

CHAIN

To work a chain stitch, begin with a slip knot on the hook. Bring the yarn **over** hook from back to front, catching the yarn with the hook and turning the hook slightly toward you to keep the yarn from slipping off. Draw the yarn through the slip knot (*Fig. 1*) (**first chain st made,** *abbreviated ch*).

Fig. 1

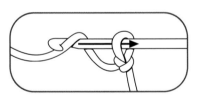

WORKING INTO THE CHAIN

When counting chains, always begin with the first chain from the hook and then count toward the beginning of your foundation chain (*Fig. 2a*).

Fig. 2a

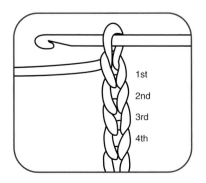

Method 1: Insert hook into back ridge of each chain (*Fig. 2b*).

Fig. 2b

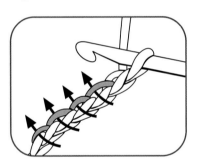

Method 2: Insert hook under top two strands of each chain (*Fig. 2c*).

Fig. 2c

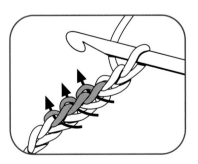

SLIP STITCH

To work a slip stitch, insert hook in stitch indicated, YO and draw through stitch and through loop on hook *(Fig. 3)* **(slip stitch made, *abbreviated slip st)*.**

Fig. 3

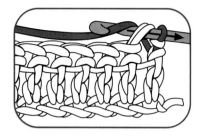

SINGLE CROCHET

Insert hook in stitch indicated, YO and pull up a loop, YO and draw through both loops on hook *(Fig. 4)* **(single crochet made, *abbreviated sc)*.**

Fig. 4

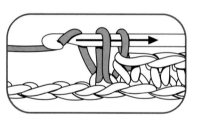

HALF DOUBLE CROCHET

YO, insert hook in stitch indicated, YO and pull up a loop, YO and draw through all 3 loops on hook *(Fig. 5)* **(half double crochet made, *abbreviated hdc)*.**

Fig. 5

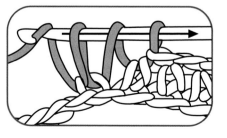

DOUBLE CROCHET

YO, insert hook in stitch indicated, YO and pull up a loop (3 loops on hook), YO and draw through 2 loops on hook *(Fig. 6a)*, YO and draw through remaining 2 loops on hook *(Fig. 6b)* **(double crochet made, *abbreviated dc)*.**

Fig. 6a   Fig. 6b

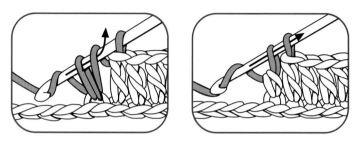

FREE LOOPS OF A CHAIN

When instructed to work in free loops of a chain, work in loop indicated by arrow *(Fig. 7)*.

Fig. 7

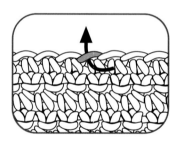

Basic Knit Stitches & Techniques

SLINGSHOT CAST ON

Step 1: Pull a length of yarn from the skein, allowing approximately 1" (2.5 cm) of yarn for each stitch to be cast on. Make a slip knot at the measured distance, pulling gently on both yarn ends to tighten the stitch on the needle.

Step 2: Hold the needle in your right hand with your index finger resting on the slip knot.

Step 3: Place the short end of the yarn over your left thumb, and bring the working yarn up and over your left index finger. Hold both yarn ends in your left palm with your 3 remaining fingers *(Fig. 8a)*.

Fig. 8a

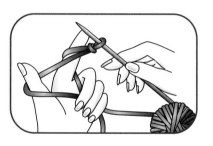

Step 4: Insert the tip of the needle **under** the first strand of yarn on your left thumb *(Fig. 8b)*.

Fig. 8b

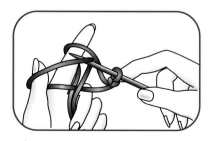

Step 5: Bring the needle **over** and around the first strand on your index finger *(Fig. 8c)*.

Fig. 8c

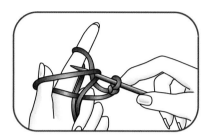

Step 6: Pull the yarn and needle down through the loop on your thumb *(Fig. 8d)*.

Fig. 8d

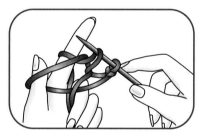

Step 7: Slip your thumb out of the loop and bring it toward you, catching the yarn end to form a new loop on your thumb *(Fig. 8e)*, and gently pulling to tighten the new stitch on the needle. Rest your right index finger on the new stitch.

Fig. 8e

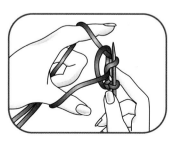

Repeat Steps 4-7 for each additional stitch.

KNIT STITCH

Step 1: Hold the needle with the cast on stitches in your left hand and the empty needle in your right hand.

Step 2: With the working yarn in **back** of the needles, insert the right needle into the stitch closest to the tip of the left needle as shown in *Fig. 9a*.

Fig. 9a

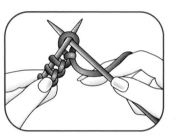

Step 3: Hold the right needle with your left thumb and index finger while you bring the yarn beneath the right needle and between the needles from back to front *(Fig. 9b)*.

Fig. 9b

Step 4: With your right hand, bring the right needle (with the loop of yarn) toward you and through the stitch *(Fig. 9c)*, slipping the old stitch off the left needle and gently pulling to tighten the new stitch on the shaft of the right needle.

Fig. 9c

PURL STITCH

Step 1: Hold the needle with the stitches in your left hand and the empty needle in your right hand.

Step 2: With the yarn in front of the needles, insert the right needle into the front of the stitch as shown in *Fig. 10a*.

Fig. 10a

Step 3: Hold the right needle with your left thumb and index finger while you bring the yarn between the needles from right to left and around the right needle *(Fig. 10b)*.

Fig. 10b

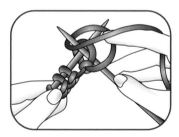

Step 4: Move the right needle (with the loop of yarn) through the stitch and away from you *(Fig. 10c)*, slipping the old stitch off the left needle and gently pulling to tighten the new stitch on the shaft of the right needle.

Fig. 10c

general instructions

42

BINDING OFF

Step 1: Knit 2 stitches.

Step 2: With the left needle, bring the first stitch over the second stitch and off the needle *(Fig. xa)*. One stitch has been bound off and one stitch remains on your right needle *(Fig. 11b)*.

Fig. 11a   Fig. 11b

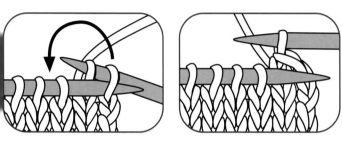

Step 3: Knit the next stitch.

Repeat Steps 2 and 3 until only one stitch remains.

Step 4: To lock the last stitch, cut the yarn (leaving a long end) and bring it up through the last stitch *(Fig. 11c)*, pulling to tighten.

Fig. 11c

YARN OVERS

After a knit stitch, before a knit stitch
Bring the yarn forward **between** the needles, then back **over** the top of the right hand needle, so that it is now in position to knit the next stitch *(Fig. 12a)*.

Fig. 12a

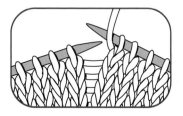

After a purl stitch, before a purl stitch
Take yarn **over** the right hand needle to the back, then forward **under** it, so that it is now in position to purl the next stitch *(Fig. 12b)*.

Fig. 12b

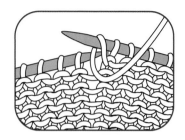

After a knit stitch, before a purl stitch
Bring yarn forward **between** the needles, then back **over** the top of the right hand needle and forward **between** the needles again, so that it is now in position to purl the next stitch *(Fig. 12c)*.

Fig. 12c

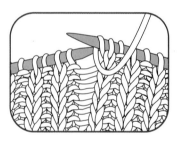

After a purl stitch, before a knit stitch
Take yarn **over** right hand needle to the back, so that it is now in position to knit the next stitch *(Fig. 12d)*.

Fig. 12d

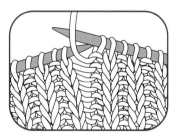

KNIT 2 TOGETHER
(abbreviated K2 tog)

Insert the right needle into the **front** of the first two stitches on the leaft needle as if to **knit** *(Fig. 13)*, then knit them together.

Fig. 13

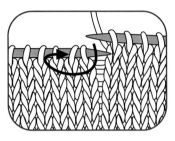

SLIP 1, KNIT 1, PASS SLIPPED STITCH OVER
(abbreviated slip 1, K1, PSSO)

Slip one stitch as if to **knit** *(Fig. 14a)*. Knit the next stitch. With the left needle, bring the slipped stitch over the knit stitch *(Fig. 14b)* and off the needle.

Fig. 14a   Fig. 14b

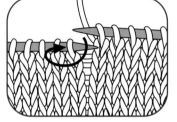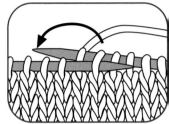

We have made every effort to ensure that these instructions are accurate and complete.
We cannot, however, be responsible for human error, typographical mistakes, or variations in individual work.

Pieces made and instructions tested by Sue Galucki and Dale Potter.

ISBN 1-57486-591-9

20 19 18 17 16 15 14

general instructions

PRINTED WITH SOY INK

Made in U.S.A.